Peachy

Angelina T. Patton

Presentation by *BookLeaf Publishing*

Web: www.bookleafpub.com

E-mail: info@bookleafpub.com

ISBN: 9789358317107

First edition 2023

For DP

Love AP

ACKNOWLEDGMENT

Thank you to: my parents Lou and Faye, who always supported my writing (sorry it took several years to publish). But especially to my mother who didn't put me in a box that said "free to a good home," even though she had every right to. My husband Dustin, thanks for always making me laugh. You are the love of my life. My children for putting up with and loving me. My brothers, Jeff and Fred, and my cousin Marianne Molendy Feller. David Moulton, the very best speech coach. To Dr. Thomas E. Emerson who taught me quite a bit about life and being an administrative professional. To Carol and Aaron Ammons, thank you for your friendship, mentoring, and support. Thank you to my Atlanta family, I love you all. The title and cover of this book are a nod to my father and mother-in-law, Phil and Nina. To my grandparents Dorothy and Vito who I never got to meet but think of every day. To my grandmother, Elsie, I still love and miss you. To my great-grandparents Ermelinda and Federico who had the courage to leave Italy for Ellis Island.

When my father died in 2019, it shook me and some of my family to the core. His presence loomed large in our lives and in different ways. When he was gone, it left a void that couldn't be filled. But I still hear his voice, in my head on days when big life events happen. And I heard his voice when I was struggling with writing. He said, "What are you afraid of? Just write the damn thing." So I did.

What It Means To Be A Woman Over 40

Shaving, exfoliating, and moisturizing.
Plucking, dyeing, and cutting.
Shampooing, conditioning, and facial masks.
Oh my god why is my skin still so fucking dry?
Filing, painting, and shaping of nails.
Menu creation, cooking, and apologizing for
mediocre meals.
Applying make-up that should show less
wrinkles and illuminates skin.

(Spoiler there is no makeup that will show less wrinkles and ain't no more light on your skin or anywhere else).
Shopping for work, lounge, and exercise clothes, and shoes.
Styling hair with products that don't work on textured hair even though the ads promised less frizz and more defined curls.
Scrolling through the socials wondering why I'm not that thin, successful, sexy, funny, or winning any mom trophies.
Helping children navigate bigger life problems, longing for the days of toddler tantrums.
Trying to stay connected to a partner, while wearing panty briefs and not a thong.
Daydreaming of leaving a country in chaos for a quieter life in Italy.
Avoiding the news and any commercials about heartburn medications' side effects.
Organizing photos, prints and digital even though you are rarely in any of said images.
Running errands wondering why I'm sweating so much when it's 52 degrees outside.
No, really why do I feel like I'm being microwaved from within?
Wanting to retire at 49 instead of 65.
Why does my back hurt all the time?
Caring for parents, and worrying why I haven't heard from so and so in a while.

Becoming increasingly aware of my invisibility
to the male species and the world.
Lighting candles, reading, and listening to
podcasts about how to be better at everything.
Running on 4 hours of sleep, thanks to
menopause.
Staying the course even when every fiber of my
being says, "I've seen everything I've needed to
see."
Trying not to let the world or cruel people make
me into a bitter old hag.
Insert Midwest "ope" here.
Too late.

Osage Orange Tree

At the end of summer we laid down on the
ground, sprawled under a tree;
We laughed and giggled, choraling kids to smile
and sit closer;
We thought this time would last forever, we all
felt so safe and free.

Under the Osage Orange Tree the photographer
snapped each pic;
Some portraits can't really show all that had to
happen to get here;
One failed marriage to a monster, someone so
careless and sick.

A portrait wouldn't show me randomly sitting
down at a bar next to my future husband;
Feeling like a lightning bolt had struck my head;

Happy you didn't listen to people who said this
would be a terribly bad end.

For a bachelor to take three little kids and a
single mom and make a family;
No, an image could never reflect the jokes,
adventures, and love we made;
One late summer day, we stopped time and laid
under the Osage orange tree.

50: Ode to the Champaign County Clerk on the Occasion of His Birthday

Always tenacious, never mendacious. Sing his praises because you've seen his phases.
Never one to hide from anything, especially the truth. Spoken word genius and the County Clerk to boot.

Don't get it mixed up, this isn't the big come up. Puttin' in work in these streets from sundown to sun up.

He is a counselor, a radical, and testifier. Clap your hands together for the grand riser!

Higher ground isn't always a given, challenge
measure by measure and change the day-to-day
livin'.
Hear the words from Dr King about longevity
having its place. Carrying the burdens and hopes
since Kiwane's life was erased.

Tireless anchor to the marginalized and
criminalized too. Serving as an inspiration and
guide for all that will see it through.

So accept this happy birthday poem from me to
you—here's to another 50–happy birthday to
you.

Matte

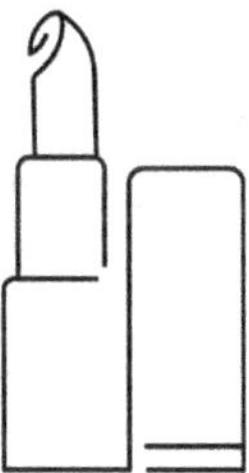

There is a lipstick I wear, Chanel Endless is the name,
Quite fitting since women are accused of having endless questions.
It's a perfect matte, a burnt orange, with rays of sun.

A sea of reds and plums fill the lip military cabinet,
Soft browns and even a bright fuscia round out the lip pallet,
But none compare to my Chanel, the consummate professional and vet.

Isn't it funny how attached I've become?
Shouldn't be too surprised, it's like a very trusted advisor and friend,

Mouth stings like venom, sharper words come
out meaning people and things have an end.

But Chanel and cigarettes have never let me
down. And so I leave my house each day ready
for war with my lipstick crown.

Even during the pandemic my mask was stained
with lipstick traces,
never ashamed and wasn't going to let COVID
win,
It was a marathon and not for the faint of heart
graces.

If I was ever stranded on an island,
And could only bring one cosmetic item,
My answer without hesitation would be to bring
my perfect matte friend.

A Theory as to Why America Can't Sleep

I think I have figured out the sleep crisis in the United States. Meaning no one is sleeping well. Between social media and 24/7 streaming services I think I've cracked the code. As I was looking at channels at 2AM when sleep was elusive this is what I discovered in the listing of shows:

Deadly Love
Snapped
Cold Case
Dateline
Dateline Secrets: Uncovered

Air Disasters
Unsolved Mysteries
The First 48
National News
Locked up: 90 days in
My 600 lb Life
Forensic Files
48 Hours
20/20 Murder in a Small Town
Sex in the City
Dial M for Murder
Killer Couples
Homicide Detectives
True Confessions
Murder She Wrote
Golden Girls
The Curse of Oak Island
Swamp People
CSI Miami
CSI Calcutta
CSI Hawaii
CSI New York
CSI: The Convent for Nuns
Mystery Diagnosis
Infomercial about an Airfryer
Infomercial about airbrush makeup
Crazy Exes
Cheaters
Cops

The Darkside of the Ring

Mind you, this is just a theory…

LT

Grief is not a linear thing. It has exposed all my weaknesses. It has shoved my knees to the ground with uncontrollable shakes and cries. It has made my face raw from tissues and wiping away tears.

The night before you died was the 75th anniversary of D-Day. All that was on the news were interviews from the handful of survivors. I was so miserable that night I thought I was dying. I was hot and restless and felt like my insides were being squeezed through a juicer. And when the phone call came that you were gone I already knew. I just wanted to pick up the phone and hear your voice. That ungodly

baritone voice. The voice that had been marred
and distorted from alcohol and cigarettes. A life
well lived.

I wish you knew all the things I found out or
realized after you were gone. All the secrets kept
and for what? Because you felt guilty? It only
made me love you more. I put you in a place
where you could be at peace. A place where you
could rejoin the family circle after all. That's
what love can do. It can repair a hole the size of
Alaska and make it better than before.

I put pictures of your real family in the box of
ashes. I didn't want you to be alone or worse,
forget what your kids looked like. I needed you
to know that everyone was devastated when you
left and I've never been the same. I know I never
will. I found pinecones at the cemetery when we
left you there. Whenever I find a stray one, I
think it's something you left me. Whenever I see
a fat red bird on my walks I think it's you. The
concert album recording you were there for in
California takes me back to a place and time
when you were alive with your whole life ahead
of you. I watch the vinyl and hear the crackling
of Errol humming.

I know later you thought jazz was just noise but
I know that deep down you still loved it. And
your grandkids love it. Erin plays Misty and my
eyes flood. Ben puts on the Errol Garner album
and a deep ache in my chest burns and my throat
clenches. It's all because I love you. It's all
because they love you.

And every time I hit a milestone or your
grandkids do I want to tell you. I want you to see
your fingerprints all over their DNA. In 2019, I
found a Christmas card you sent in 2015 saying
you wish we could all be together again eating
tortellini. We did. All of us came together that
Christmas after you died. We ate and cried. We
went to mass and cried. It's all because I love
you. It's all because they love you and always
will. You're still my favorite person, it's me, it's
me, it's Angie T.

To DP from AP

It was an unusually warm March in 2004. The fields had shoved tulips to the front of the Spring pageant to be crowned the winners. A park divided us and we took the long way round.

Both of us knew this was it for us. No other could compare, nor anyone could understand it was destiny. It is in fact, the stuff poets and dreamers write about. I was a very lapsed Catholic. Funny how that all turned out.

Loving you has been easy, you loving me has been hard in a lot of ways. I came out of the box broken. It's not your fault. But you still get me like no other. You always know how to handle me. It's absurd that we can read each other's minds. Just one look, and you know if I want to sneak cigarettes or scowl that tells you I'm done with this conversation.

But REAL love is not grand gestures of flowers or jewelry. True love is a lot less sexy. It's comforting your spouse after a parent dies. It's spending weekends at kids' sporting events. It's doing laundry and cooking when someone is melting into the floor and overwhelmed. It's quietly making the other person a better version of themselves. It's holding hands at the end of the night when both man and wife are equally exhausted. It's taking someone for granted and being forgiven when they didn't deserve it. It's knowing that we will never be separated. That death or time can't break this connection. It's knowing we will always find ourselves together again and again, in this life and in the next.

Guns by the River

They went hunting one beautiful day. Guns and dogs in tow. The dogs barking added more chaos than usual. Two friends who went down by the river to hunt quail and anything else they could kill. There was tension in the air.

A friend lured him there under the guise of hunting. It seemed like a perfect set up. The road to hell is paved with questionable intentions.

Buck shot! The rifle rang out.
Buck shot again! Dead silence.

Oh no. Ohhh no. The friend collapsed. The other hunter called his pa in a panic. He had actually done what he had set out to do. Immediate remorse and grief made his head pound. He gathered leaves and tried to cover up his friend. He became hysterical waiting for the cavalry to arrive.

His father pulled up in an old pick up truck. A truck that was once his own father's, who died under suspicious circumstances in a wreck near the Mill River. Old Kodak pictures revealed the crash and they covered it with a dark muddy tarp when they had the funeral for his father. The pictures looked like they had an Instagram filter added to them. He shook off the memory and stepped out of the agonizing past. Not believing he was feeling that history was repeating itself.

Slap!
Slap!

Yelling Goddamns and what were you thinking? More stupids and assholes were shouted out.. You've ruined everything.

Tears stung the hunter's eyes as unhinged sobbing came.

Lucky for him his father knew the sheriff and the state's attorney. They summoned both after getting their stories straight. It was an accident. He wasn't where he was supposed to be and wasn't wearing his vest.

The sheriff delivered the news to the victim's family. Typical sorry for your loss and there was no chance of saving him. The family knew there was more to the story but there was no point in protesting. Not when everyone was in the same bed together. Meaning the authorities.
The girl the fight was over came to the funeral. She wept, never imagining it would come to this. She left town shortly after. Rumors swirled at the school, coffee shop, and grocery store about her being a slut and she was all to blame. Strange since she never owned a gun. Her parents arranged for her to go to the city where the convent would take care of her and her unborn baby. Only she knew who the father was. And he was dead, down by the river.

Briar Foxes

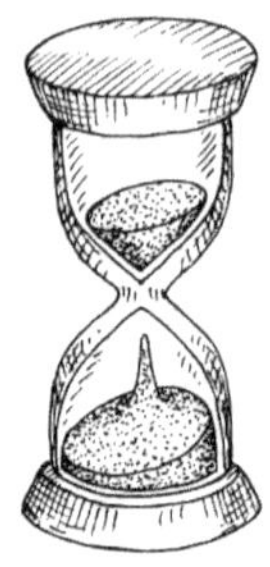

She sings lullabies with a soft southern lilt about briar foxes getting me if I don't go to sleep. She rocks and pats and prays the colic is relieved. She wonders why she had a baby at 35 that would stretch and break her in ways she could never prepare for. Stubborn and silly child that looks and acts just like her daddy. So unfair. She wanted a girl that would dress up and be a lady just like her. It was very unfair.

Only to have *that* daddy leave her for a new love he found. This happened right after her mother had died of brain cancer. Incurable. A summer spent caring for and wiping up after her own mother. Leaving her own family to care for her mother. After the words "terminal" were uttered it was the first time I saw you cry. We stood at the trunk of the car. I didn't know what to do,

but it registered that you were human. A
beautifully strong human for everyone. Putting
everyone before yourself. It was very unfair.

That summer in Milltown I played with my
cousin and sang to the *Footloose* soundtrack. We
played with our Barbies and couldn't grasp that
our Grandmother was slipping further away. She
didn't suffer long. But it was very unfair. We
didn't know anything was wrong until she
burned the green beans on the stove. I can still
imagine her kitchen, with black rod iron chairs
and a diner-esque table in the middle. The
window looked out over the garden. I would sell
my soul for her fried chicken and pickled beets.
Daddy didn't like such southern cooking, but we
loved the peach cobbler. 8 children she had, 7
survived. Raising a family on a dairy farm. It
was very unfair. But she would never see it that
way.

She was proud of her life and her daughter that
cared for her in those dark times. She was proud
of all her grandchildren. She would crochet
house slippers and spend hours on the phone
with her favorite daughter. Just like we do now.
You're still my favorite person to talk to. Sorry I
was so difficult when I was young. I just didn't
know what I was mad about and it took me a

while to figure it out. It was very unfair to you. But I still think about you singing me to sleep with Briar Foxes waiting to get me when I don't sleep.

Gamekeeper

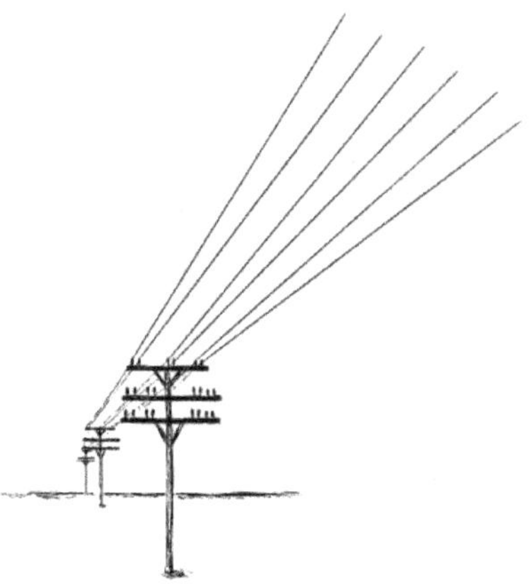

I see the cows along First Street against the backdrop of a spectacular purple and orange sunrise. It must be my forefathers who were dairy farmers that are the reason I feel so affectionate toward these black furry bovines. I smile each time. They remind me of Erin when she was a baby, so excited to see them on the way to school.

I think of my Grandmother and her in a dress working, cooking, and milking all those cows. Never complaining, there was no need. Married to a man she met in Detroit. She was a chef. He would come in each day because he only liked her cooking. In this instance, he did in fact, marry her for her cooking. Funny now to think his family didn't think she was good enough. Had eight children at home. All natural with maybe a shot of whiskey to see her through.

Placed her babies in a dresser drawer to serve as a crib. Back then they made do with what they had. Grew their own food. On Sundays, she would fry fish and the whole town would come. Her pies sold for various causes. My grandfather made sure everyone knew his wife made the pies, he was so proud. I can still see her face framed with silver and black curls. It made me long to have brown eyes like her, like my mother.

I named my daughter after her mother, Emma. I adored that name before it was popular. My great-grandmother was a nurse and would read tea leaves and peel apples by the bushel. My mother would do the same as I sat around her feet. One single peel in a pie pan. She put salt on the slices and it was warm and sweet.

I have my mother's hair and her legs. If I had to pick two features, that isn't a bad place to land. But I am my father's daughter. Loud, funny, with features that scream Italian. The Roman nose, the *bocca*, the curves and the use of my hands always when I speak. I know no other way. At mass when they summon the faithful departed I always think of Ermelinda, Nono, Vito, and of course my father. I feel them and the incense summons their hearts. For there is still a little girl that desperately wants to see their faces.

My mother told me when I was just a little over a year old I went to my great-grandmother's funeral mass. She shook my little foot before she died, weeping because she wouldn't get to see me make my way in the world. Oh, but I could never forget you. I make tortellini in your apron and with your bowls and linens. I cry when I eat them because your great-great-grandchildren love them too. They know you and know you're always here with us.

All of these fierce women I come from. Distantly related to Ulysses S. Grant. General is what they call me now. And they aren't wrong. If I had known this pedigree sooner, I would have had a much higher opinion of myself when I was younger.

Womb

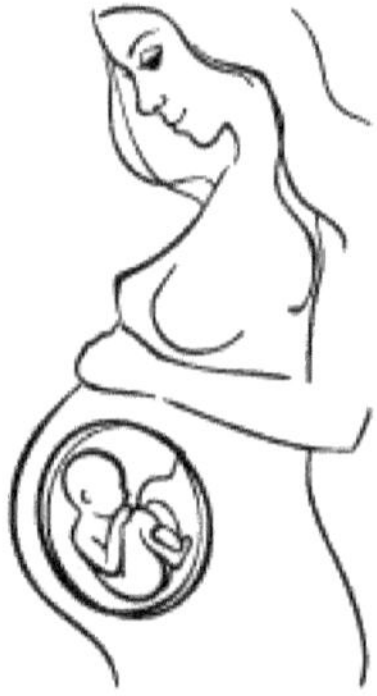

It's your birthday today. Just like the bible says, I knew you before you were ever conceived. I knew what your face would look like. Not even a conehead could prevent me from identifying you as my own. But that was many moons and a husband ago. I did the very best I could, that I promise. And yet it wasn't good enough.

You were always way too quiet. But I loved that. I was too when I was young. To the point they thought there was a hearing or speech problem. I was always in my own head just like you. You were the first kid that made me laugh at something they said. Not because it was cute. But because you said something razor-sharp and funny.

The day you left was like a bomb went off. The basement looked like a refugee camp. It wasn't because you left, that I was furious. It was because you didn't tell me. And you didn't tell me you were so unhappy. I would have fixed or supported whatever. One day you will realize that parents are just people too. Trying to figure it all out so you don't wind up like one of us.

But we are exactly alike. Scared and funny.

Soft Kisses in Tender Places

There was nothing ever tender about you. The only thing you ever said that was true, was that I was beautiful. I remember you talking about your ex-wife when she was in her thirties and you were grossed out because her legs had cellulite. I laughed nervously. At 21, there was no way that I could possibly imagine that. I was a size 6. And was so disgusted by my body. But if I had that body now I would never feel that way.

It's startling to Google your name and see the FBI report. No one believed me for so long that I was living in a solitary hell with you. It took 6 years. But they closed in and you went to prison.

You thought for so long the laws of humanity and society mean nothing. You did as you pleased until all the depravity saw the light of day.

And then you went on to your 5th wife. No shit. Can you believe that? 5th? It wasn't me. It was you all along. I don't know how I survived. I remember you sitting on my chest when I had just had Ben. I took you back one last time and you almost killed me. You tried to destroy me but I found myself along the way. I found happiness and true love. You were just some old stupid asshole that fucked his sister because he really wanted to fuck his mom.

But you will die as someone not knowing your own children and that's exactly what you deserve. You deserve to rot in hell under three thousand suns. If someone held a gun to my head I couldn't remember a single point of happiness. I only remember the horrible times and when the kids were born. As if I was alone when it all happened. But you were there. Waiting for an idiot to believe all of your lies. And when people ask me would I have married you if I had it to do over again, the answer is always the same. YES. Because of the children I got to have. And those kids' kids are all really smart and gorgeous. And they look and act like me.. Maybe I did it all myself, after all.

31

Betty Ruth

An unremarkable life for someone so remarkable. Everything I learned about makeup I learned from her. She was short and petite. There was something about her face that hid a lot of pain and hard times. She wore Avon and thought that was really cool. The one picture I remember of you is with purple tinted glasses and eyeshadow to match. Your cigarette case was leather–a smoky caramel color. The brass closure was chipped and faded.

You liked to play cards and listen to country music. Bingo too. Once when I was 10 you were talking about your boyfriends and dating challenges as an older woman, you exclaimed, "I just hate those wobbly dicks!" You were always wild, my mother said. She said you almost died of pneumonia. You were the baby born after Mildred died, and your mom couldn't bear to lose another. She let you run wild because that's just how you were made.

My mother feared I was exactly like you. You are the only aunt on my mother's side of things that my dad asked about. He said you and Gerald Wayne were so funny, and you had fun drinking and carrying on. I remember my parents drinking A LOT and having people over when I was younger. We both loved boys and doing exactly the opposite of what we were supposed to be doing. Restless and bored. And too smart for our own good. I always wondered how upset you were when your mother died. She took care of your twins when they locked you up. It wasn't your fault. I'm almost positive crazy runs on both sides now. Well, actually I am positive. But I loved you and always loved seeing you. And now I know why you never wanted to come to family reunions. But goddamn I wish I had been there when you told Robin to stop singing, "Daddy's Secret." That song was dedicated to my Uncle Jim (her father) because he had a kid no one knew about. That secret showed up at a funeral. I would have liked to have been there for that day too.

You were the coolest and funniest. My mom misses you but I call her and try to make her laugh. Last time I saw her she told me the story about when you all stayed up at the house on Gettysburg Court that you were talking about men. You told my grandmother that all Gerald Wayne "wanted to do was ride you." She laughed but didn't comment. My mother howled. Mom also told me about the time you showed up at the Masonic Temple for some formal and when you were introduced with your brother you said, "This is my brother Jim, he beats us." And they nearly fell through the floor. And *that* is exactly why I loved you.

Alright

I managed to make it out the other side of a darkness that I thought would last forever. But every storm eventually runs out of rain. I stayed in the boat and thought it would get better. I lost and found myself over and over. Realizing that I have two lives and the second one begins once I knew I only had one to live.

I was so broken, confused about what love really was. Thinking it was what came through a social media feed. I needed more but the things I really needed were in my face all along. I was so worried about having a mid-life crisis play out, that I didn't even recognize my own.

But it's never too late. I remembered the best advice from my mother and father. It went something like this:

The least said is the easiest mended.
Don't piss on my boot and tell me it's raining.
Other than that Mrs. Lincoln, how did you like the play?
It's a piece of shit all the way around.
Your actions speak so fucking loud, I can't hear a fucking word you are saying.
But, anyway…
Don't take sides against your family.
A hot shower will fix a lot of things.
Laughter is THE best medicine.
You can't lose what you never had.
The world will try to grind you down and break you in a million different ways, but don't let it make you bitter.
Grief is the price of loving someone deeply.
Opinions are like assholes…
Tend to your own knitting.

Don't take it personally…I'm unsure how else to
take it.
Making tortellini heals broken hearts and brings
a family together, no matter what.

Every Now and Then

I run to the old vices every now and then,
The things that make me cope,
The preacher would debate vices or sin?

All my life I've waited for something and never
planned,
Drifting from one questionable decision to
another. Time is an abstract like grains of sand.

I realize now that I am a bottomless pit of need,
I wonder if you really love me, scared of the
answer,
I never ask, I get enough slack to not feel so
much greed.

I look at the mirror and still feel like the same
insecure girl I was at 17,
Makeup and accessories only hide so much,
The eyes always give away the parts I don't
want seen.

Isn't everyone searching for something, if not
money and fame,
It's the capital society's way,
I kid myself and say I'm different, but really it's
the same.
All the stories and issues I carry can't be for not,
Who cares you're on the crux of 50,
A thief in the night, seconds go by and I
understand the clear life and lot.

I don't want to have anxiety and second guess,
When I know what I'm capable of,
Even if at times it seems very suspicious.

Every now and then I seek the things that once
brought me comfort,
Attention, cigarettes, shopping, the direct
opposite of your cravings,
My ideas and notions are a struggle to sort.

But every now and then I fight the good fight
and do what I'm supposed to,
Crawling and scrapping all along the way,

Relief is temporary just like prayers, wishes, and
voodoo.

If all it took was to cast a spell,
I most certainly would light a candle with
crystals to frame,
But instead I'm stuck inside my head, also
known as hell.

Not Even a Poet

I'm not a poet and that is sure to see,
I know all the rules, but much like in life,
I don't think they apply to me.

All the words and phrases stuck inside my head,
Like a constant running narrative of things lost
and found,
And not enough time to do the thing that keeps
me fed.

No, I'm not a poet as anyone can see,
But that doesn't mean that I don't have a writer's
heart and soul,
A caged bird longing to be free.

When I think of poets, I think of old women
with frizzy hair,
Wooden jewelry and jean jumpers to decorate
their frame,
I don't think I fit that mold, and honestly, I do
not care.

When I think of poets, I think of Victorian
ruffles and white petticoats,
I think of people in black turtlenecks and berets,
But I'm none of those things either, because I'm
someone who has sowed wild oats.

No, I'm not a poet, and even Stevie Wonder
could see,
That my writing doesn't fit convention or style,
And honestly, that's just fine by me.

But don't you dare say that my words don't
matter,
That they don't carry weight or worth,
I just think writers, in general, have to be
somewhat mad as a hatter.

So you see, the words I string together are
what's in my heart and mind,
They come to me at dawn or dusk, or when I
least expect it,

But they mean more than I could say or show,
and the truest love I find.

RiverValley

There's a place we go sometimes in the summer
and for new year,
A place that is very special, we hold dear.
A place that was a mystery for many months,
A warm and welcoming home, a bond between
father and son.

Some would say a mistake, others knowing
better,
That no one is the real author of life, no goal
getter.
A family reunited by an angel,
Out of the sky, her Nini would say, she did fell.

A pool made of water and peaches,
DNA matches crossing far reaches.
A paternity no one could deny,
A hope and glimmer of his father's eye.

The road was long traveled and well worth the
wait,
A red caravan did pull up into the driveway gate.
A letter sent with pictures to share,
A response that was honest and fair.

Baby had just learned to walk that summer and
around the table she did go,
Unphased by the reunion of souls, consumed
with not letting the past show.
A stranger came to the house and a member he
did leave,
A story so strange you would have to see to
believe.

But seeing isn't always believing,
Unasked questions, with little grieving.
Answers given and messages sent,
Weekly phone calls and holidays spent.

Now the baby that toddled around the table is a
student at college,
Making her way back home before the last
falling of foliage.
Airplane visits to and fro,
It's hard to believe she is so grown.

No one would have fathomed, reasoned, or
guessed,

That something so painful, could be so blessed.
In every way, song and sound,
It will always be a second home of love found.

A northerner who traveled through the civil war
tragedy,
To grasp at something, desperately needed.
A man who defined nature vs. nurture,
No one could predict this future.
For in situations such as this,
There's a lot one could miss.

I know that love cannot be defined by time or
space,
Although others could make a different case,
Of similar circumstances with matching faces
and names,
Incredible how much you do share, in face and
grains.

Stubborn, strong, and picky,
Not in a hurry, but sometimes quickly.
Southern cooking and booze to pass,
Family dinners and a saint's Saturday mass.

Milestones big and hidden,
Riding lessons on morning ridden.
All boys and one older girl,
Rounding out the next generation's unfurl.

Those who know, actually do know,
Deeply tender feelings on both sides do show.
A reunion of souls they greet,
A match destined to meet.

Beloved family at RiverValley,
The memories made are far too many to tally.
A special place that house will always be,
Atlanta family we do love thee.

These Hands

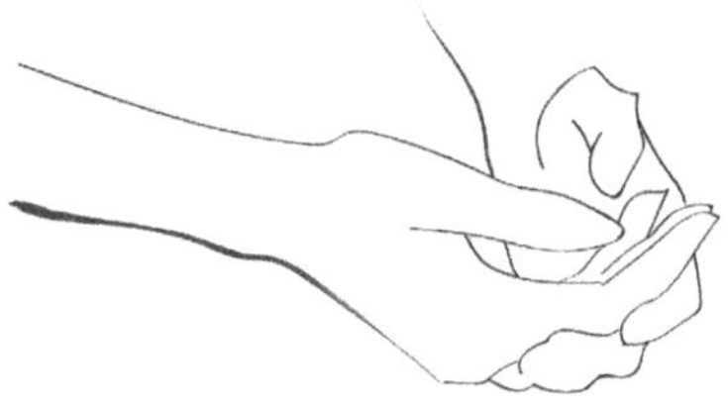

I remember holding my father's enormous hands when I was a little girl. They made me feel safe and free. I remember when I first noticed my own hands didn't resemble my mother's in any way, shape or form.

My mother's hands were long and elegant, they still are.
My hands are those of the women on my father's side of the family.
Strong, tan, with just the slightest orange tint on my finger from a smoking habit I can't quite kick.

My daughters' hands are soft and elegant-both very different from one another. My oldest has baby hands, which we've teased her about. She would quickly admit it's true. My youngest daughter has an artist's hands. They look like her aunts and I love that about them.

The youngest and I share a writer's callus. I'll
never forget the day when we were examining
our hands and comparing as people do. She was
so relieved to see the calloused bump on the
middle finger we both share. Formed by
pressure, putting pen to paper in the ways that
we do.

No one in the history of ever has commented on
the beauty of my hands, except for my oldest
daughter. She would say, "I love your hands,"
and almost admonish me for my disdain over
this feature. But I came to realize what she was
really saying.

These are the hands that she knows and has
memorized, just like me with my father's hands.
These are the ones that would tell her it's really
me, and could easily identify out of a lineup.
These hands have rocked and patted her, they
have scolded and brought great comfort too.

And while there is no controlling, what my
hands would look like. I do take comfort in the
fact, they are distinctly mine. They have done
things, big and small. They have waged war and
fought against a lot of dark things. They can

open jars with ease and pick up pieces when
they fall.

They can catch things as they are about to slip
through the cracks. They make things whole
again. They are mine and I have reconciled all
the things I used to hate about them. But I am so
glad I have two daughters that have the most
beautiful and feminine hands I have ever seen.

Feast at a Funeral

They laid you to rest today, and many came to
view,
The remains of what was left of you.
Not much to look at with bald patches of hair,
But it didn't stop them from their stare.

They came from far and wide to see you lying
there peaceful and still,
They came from your own hometown, the river
with a mill.
Your blue dress and casket were all decked out,
The undertaker even made you look presentable,
no one could doubt.

My mother wept, and I'm not sure of why,
Perhaps the reminder that time is fleeting and it
made her cry.

She said nice things, even though you didn't
deserve,
Making her feel badly about everything, boy,
you had some nerve.

I always wonder what a preacher will say when
someone like you dies,
Are people really upset, or are those tears lies?
If people could say what they really wanted to,
Would they say you were an old and selfish
fool?

Oh, the things I wanted to say and shout,
The things that I knew and could have said-but I
went a different route.
I sat there going through funeral traditions
unmoved and still,
Knew that you were bitter and miserable at the
end- just like in your life's fill.

But as they say back home,
It's all over but the shoutin' as they laid you
down in a dirt dome.
Nothing left to say or do,
A new and warm afterlife for you.

There aren't shoes or shopping where you are
now,

No orders or missives to direct, no permission to
allow.
You came in with nothing and couldn't take it
with you when you left,
The deeds you will have to answer for, things
that made your dearest bereft.

I think there is a special place in hell for those
who go out of their way to hurt others,
But I'm no judge, jury, or your mother.
Funny, the only thing they could say is you
wanted your service over and quick,
The inside was just as ugly as the outside-broken
and sick.

But your finale was unremarkable and the
graveside too,
Stones emerging from the earth, announcing an
adieu.
All indistinguishable from the rest,
When you get to where you're going, we send
our very best.

There won't be greeters or a welcome mat,
Only the dark, in silence falling flat.
No trumpets or angel with arms open,
Only the still compost and erosion.

Dreams aren't what you'll have,

Time stands there, no hurry to run off to or dash.
Leaving the earth forever,
Everyone was relieved, ties permanently
severed.

Queen Bees

What makes a bee, a queen? Is it the stripes or
size?
Is it the attitude and authority? Or being a boss
to all the guys?
Their honey the sweetest, a tribute to their
throne,
A real lesson in work ethic, killin' them off with
no thought to atone.

Beautiful crown the queen bee wears,
All the workers in the hive, she has no real care.

Except to make sure they buzz and the
honeycomb they keep,
No time for rest, no time for sleep.

Working them night and day,
No wonder their time is not a long stay.
Morning and night you hear the buzz,
Disarming, with her shocking yellow and black
fuzz.

She doesn't hide and is easy to spot in any
crowd,
Having to do what needs to be done, never
hiding in a shroud.
She's elegant with arms and legs to spare,
Death is the price you pay as a worker, she will
charge you a fare.

The workers look up with adoring eyes,
To the queen they worship, there is no loyalty or
family ties.
For once their work is done and they are no
longer of use,
Each one is murdered off in a frenzy of bee
abuse.

The Queen Bees know exactly who they are and
what they want.

They dream of flowers that serve a summer
flaunt.
This bee isn't satisfied with leaves or stem,
Only flowers with its revealing stamen.

There is nothing that can hold her back,
With the prize in her sights, picking up slack.
Creating her city on the comb,
No worker bee realizing, this is their tomb.

There will always be a Queen Bee in every life,
Whether it's a foe, friend, or wife.
Queens exist for every season,
These glorious supermodels of nature give us
many reasons.
To love and admire,
To begin the burst of Spring's colorful fire.

Peachy

Peachy is a state the color of coral,
Muddy river waters that were once immoral.
Nestled in the arms of the civil war,
Confusing highways and stars.

Peachy is a state of being,
A misunderstood phrase when greeting.
Crowds gather at roadside stands,
Looking for perfect peaches in hands.

Peachy is a nickname for those who wish you well,
A state in the south, hotter than the flames of hell.
Humidity so thick you could cut with a knife,
Married families, husband and wife.

Peachy is in the land of cotton,

Where history will never be forgotten.
School field trips with bee colored busses,
Where Dixie isn't whistled, nor is it fussy.

White glove tea parties and bows in hair,
Generational wealth on display without care.
Where colors of purple and gold do live,
Music and entertainers with much to give.
Peachy is many things to many people,
Peachy is the name of this piece, my writer's
steeple.
Round and beautiful with soft hair to bare,
Peachy it is, peachy so charming and fair.

Holiday Song Titles from TikTok (if a new artist was releasing their Christmas album on TikTok)

You Better Sleigh Ho!

These Elves Stand on Business

I Saw Mommy Kissing Mrs. Claus to Go Viral

Rizz in a Manger

O Little Town of Vibe Check

Frosty the Sus Snowman

Holly Extra Christmas

No Cap Christmas

Z'at You Salty Claus?

Stop Fat Shaming Frosty the Snowman

Rudolph Needs to Be Cancelled!

12 Days of Gaslighting

Dasher and Dancer are Toxic This Time of Year

VJT

I look for you in WWII documentaries. I search for you in my memories. Mostly through the scraps of personal items you left your son. An Army duffle bag, your dog tags in a tall, cylinder, silver, salt shaker. A wood box nailed shut. It wasn't until after your son died that I looked through the box of negatives. It had vintage postcards and maps from Europe and the college you went to. The old envelopes from photo developing were in their original packaging and meticulously organized.

I'm not sure what I was expecting when I developed the negatives into digital files. You were so handsome and tall. So many pictures were so intimate I felt as if I shouldn't be looking at them. One of the photos in the series had a slight young brunette in a knit dress. Hair curled and make-up faded from a swim and picnic by the lake. It looked like a romantic Sunday for two lovers. You had her arm around her waist and were pulling her close. She was looking straight ahead, but you were looking at her like you might just devour her. I wanted so badly to know her name. I wished out loud that I wanted someone to look at me like you were looking at her in the photograph.

All your son ever said about you was that you were devastatingly handsome. That you were ridiculously smart. That you drank and when you drank too much you were mean. I stood over the wooden box removing your graduation program and Army discharge papers. The graduation program listed your name as Veto instead of Vito. Vito Joseph, you were the Salutatorian. The Army discharge papers showed faithful service and an honorable discharge after your tour through the Rhineland Campaign in Germany. I wondered what happened to you over in Europe. As I grew up, I came to realize the things that your son didn't say. That you were a first generation American. That your parents immigrated from Lizzano, Italy to the harbor of Ellis Island. The crowned blue woman with welcoming arms. That you went to fight for a country that didn't really care about immigrants. That you were fighting your home country. That the Battle of the Bulge was arguably one of the most significant moments within the WWII timeline.

But you came home a changed person. You had two sons, and one you denied. You divorced your wife and married someone else. You were so young when you died, only 44. I can still Google the headline of your obituary, still jarring to see. You died on the job as a railway mail clerk. I cannot imagine the agony of your mother when the priest wouldn't come to give you last rights. That you wouldn't have a Catholic funeral. That you would be separated for eternity from your family. A headstone resides at Marengo City Cemetery, one space for your then wife, your name next to hers. But she wasn't buried there. She moved on, but not everyone did.

Your sister was devastated, your mother racked
with grief. Your son, her only reminder. Your
son would stand at the fireplace and look at your
picture and cry. Was it because of the
relationship he wished he had? Was it because
there wasn't enough time together? Your son
died when I was 45 and I didn't feel like I had
enough time. All the questions I wanted to ask
him about you and his life. All of it came after
his death. And now all we have is beautiful
photos in black and white of the statue of David,
the Louvre, nameless Army buddies who you
served with, and intimate personal photos of
love you shared. How is it possible to feel so
connected to someone I have never met? I visit
your family at Ascension, where I put your son
next to your sister. Right between your parents.
It's where you belong too. But I believe we will
all be reunited again one day. That when my
time is done on this Earth, that you will be
waiting on the shore to greet me. It will be a
bright and sunny day with the ocean in the
background. I will see your mother and father
and I will run to them. You will have your arms
open, you will be standing next to your son, my
father, and I will get to see both of your faces.
One face for the first time, and the other face
again.

Isn't it Funny?

He's so funny and irreverent!

I remember as we neared Christmas in 2022, a friend of mine and I decided to go to see a famous author do a reading of his material and then waited for hours so he could sign our books. It was a fun girls evening, a fun dinner, some wine, and an exchanging of gifts. You were one of my favorite authors, I would put you in the same category as Christopher Hitchens, which is the top tier writer category for me. You stepped out on stage to show off your outfit. So very eclectic and so very proud

of what you chose to wear to a venue at a sleepy
little college town in the Midwest. You read to
us works that were published and soon to be.
Rattling off that the New Yorker was going to
publish this piece soon. That another piece was
going to be an essay in your upcoming book.

We laughed and we laughed some more. You
told stories about your dad who just died and
your sister too. I thought the stories were
humorous but felt uneasy when you were talking
about your dad. I always feel like people who
aren't here to defend themselves shouldn't be
fair game. I felt my stomach sink when you
talked about your sister who committed suicide.
How she was troubled and how she committed
suicide. How does *THAT* end up in a book
tour/comedy routine.

*How sad his dad passed away and his sister
committed suicide.*

The show wrapped up and everyone made their
way to form a line so you could sign books. We
brought our books and carried them with our
coats in a very hot and long line. If only I had
known then that staying in the line would be a
total disaster. My friend and I were one of the
last ones to get signatures. We heard you engage

other fans and were excited for our turn. You did mine first, I can't even remember what I said but I remember feeling like the conversation was weird and you seemed annoyed. It was clear you were ready for the evening to be over.

He always stays until the last book is signed!

You took the book signing slip from my book. I wanted it for my brother, a signed copy of the book from his sister. A funny little, "To Fred, Your sister is the best." You looked at the request and placed it to the side. You grabbed red and black markers. You started to write, no, carve the words, "To Fred, Your sister is a WHORE." Oh my fucking God. Am I seeing this correctly? It was late and I thought, maybe I wasn't seeing what I was actually seeing. Oh fuck. You took the black marker and started to outline the word WHORE as if it wasn't prominent enough. I did what I always do in situations like that, I started laughing. But it wasn't funny. I wanted the floor to open and swallow me whole. I felt so fucking stupid. I actually bought tickets and books for this?

That's just his brand of humor! He's funny like that!

You signed my friend's book next. I'm sure she had a pit in her stomach as she watched what happened to my autographed copy. I'm sure she knew that since we came to the table as a pair that she was in for the same. And you didn't disappoint. You did give her the same treatment, you wrote "You're a WHORE too!" What the actual fuck is happening. She laughed nervously too and made small talk about her job. You ridiculed her for that too. We left the book signing line stunned and silent. Then we were laughing but neither of us thought it was funny. We sat in the car for a moment completely shocked. And for the record, I can take a joke. I'm not clutching my pearls in a fake insulted state.

I couldn't let go of what happened. Mainly because I felt like it was just mean. I called the venue and told them what happened. Nobody cared. For some reason this sleepy little college town thinks you coming here is the peak of culture. I then did what I always do in situations like this, I started to investigate. I could not be the only female that had a book signed like that. And guess what? I wasn't wrong.

"Your mother should have had an abortion."

The internet was chalked full of horror stories
where you signed women's books like that.
Funny it was only women. I saw where he
wrote, Your Mother Should Have Had an
Abortion." Super funny right? He wrote that
another woman was a whore in Minnesota. He
claims what he writes is much funnier or better
than what he's asked to write. Ah yes, you're a
genius writer who is so funny that you call
women whores. You bragged to Terri Gross that
in 2013 you wrote something really filthy in a
woman's book and she got really upset and
called a bunch of people. Obviously it didn't
detour you in any way.

"I hope you get diabetes some day."

And the thing is I laugh all the time. I even
laugh at myself, ALL. THE. TIME. Laughing is
one of my favorite things in the whole world.
But it wasn't funny. It took me and my friend
back to a time where others were mean to us and
called us names like that or tried to degrade us
for no reason at all. It felt fairly humiliating to
wait in line for two and half hours only to be
called whores. But I bet you knew that when you
signed the books that way. I came home and told
my family what happened. They were in the
same state of disbelief as I was. Yes, some

people said it's part and parcel for you to write
horrible shit in their books and that your fans
like it. Spoiler, they don't. Nobody wants to be
called a whore by an author, that up until that
point, they really enjoyed.

When I told my brother the story, reclaiming it
and making it actually funny. My brother
laughed and then felt bad. He loves that I went
to a book signing, and got a book signed by you,
despite what you did. But you are a petty cunt
and should probably stop doing that at book
signings. Especially to women who have been
ground down by the world.

Building A Library in My Mind

I'm building a library in my mind,
One page at a time.
A time capsule if you will,
Of all the ways time turns to fill.

Of seconds squandered,
Steps and trails I've wandered.
Rainy days and subtle winds,
Upended lives, and hearts to mend.

Childhood sheltered and shuttered,
Mother shouting cautions and other well
meaning things uttered.
Holiday meals and presents wrapped,

Father finishing year-end work with night's
capped.

Of boys and gentleman kissed,
Over two decades of wedded bliss.
One actual walk down a beachy aisle,
Many mistakes over many a mile.

Children carried and delivered,
Nursed and tucked, no bonds severed.
Friends and parents lost along the way,
Nothing in this world can permanently stay.

And when I leave this earthly realm, I will take
my stacks of memories,
Rolling shelves of volumes as vast as the seas.
Of all my times here that were delightful and
spoiled,
Of times when I was ecstatic and times when my
anger boiled.

When I stopped and started,
When I had to figure out ways for the soul to
barter.
All the family lore I know and is sealed,
The book of sayings could possibly reveal.

And so will go my philosophy and advice,
Things that are only known to me by sacrifice.

And now it's my job to make the books on the
shelf,
Known to all, and not just myself.

Magic in Memphis

Down in Memphis I met a King, a Killer, a Wolf, A Rocket, A Bluesmaker, A Man in Black, and the man that conducted them all. A symphony in the south, where the corners of the Mississippi River meet. Nestled away from the noise of the country, around bodies of water and mud. I sat at the altar on 706 Union Street.

Where the sun shone bright against the littered streets. Where dreams were made by fumbling and figuring out their craft. Before they even realized it was a craft. They gave us the blueprint to the future of American music. Before fame and gossip of deeds seen and unseen. Where the Confederacy took gasping breaths. A place where lyrics and rhythm were stolen and sold. Where chivalry died. Where a boy made a record for his Mama. Where a man sang about a new car that was a rocket and never got the credit he deserved.

Where a secretary found the most beautiful King
and gave him away to the world. Where he went
on to record more songs and become a movie
star. The man who ran out of time and was the
first to do it ALL. Where X marks the spot.
Where divots in the floor remain from a
thumping bass. Where future stars still want
some of that Memphis magic and conjure ghosts
from yesteryear. They pray for the perfect song
and that their luck won't fade.

The future stars write at night when the sky is
black and stars are covered by clouds. They give
tours during the day, hoping for their break. But
sometimes history can't be repeated. Sometimes
the stars perfectly align and you capture
lightning in a bottle only once. Down in
Memphis they did something that the world has
yet to see again. But we have the music from
that tiny recording studio. We see the foundation
on which rock was built. May it never roll away.
Amen.

www.ingramcontent.com/pod-product-compliance
Lightning Source LLC
LaVergne TN
LVHW011050200726
843509LV00011B/1380